ISBN 978-1-330-46786-2
PIBN 10065673

For support please visit www.forgottenbooks.com

1 MONTH OF
FREE
READING

at
www.ForgottenBooks.com

By purchasing this book you are eligible for one month membership to ForgottenBooks.com, giving you unlimited access to our entire collection of over 700,000 titles via our web site and mobile apps.

To claim your free month visit:
www.forgottenbooks.com/free65673

THINKING FOR RESULTS

By
CHRISTIAN D. LARSON

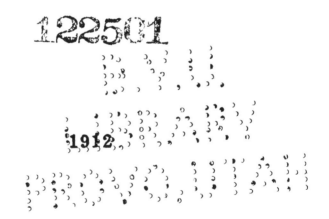
THE NEW LITERATURE
PUBLISHING COMPANY

Los Angeles

P. F. PETTIBONE & CO.
Printers and Binders
Chicago

Thinking for Results

HAT man can change himself, improve himself, recreate himself, control his environment and master his own destiny is the conclusion of every mind who is wide-awake to the power of right thought in constructive action. In fact, it is the conviction of all such minds that man can do practically anything within the possibilities of the human domain when he knows how to think, and that he can secure almost any result desired when he learns how to think for results.

Man is as he thinks he is, and what he does is the result of the sum total of his thought. The average person, however, thinks at random and therefore lives at random and does not know from day to day whether good or evil lies in his path. What he finds in his path is invariably the result of his own thinking, but as he does not know what results different kinds of thought produce he creates both good and evil daily not knowing that he necessarily does either of these. When he knows what each mental state will produce, however, and has gained the power to think as he likes under all sorts of circumstances, then he will have fate, destiny, environment, physical conditions, mental conditions, attainments, achievements and in fact everything in his own hands.

It is a well known fact that we can produce any effect desired when we understand causes, and can master those causes. And as the process of thinking is the one underlying cause in the life of man we naturally become master over all life when we can understand and master the process of thinking. Each process of thinking produces its own results in mind and body and acts indirectly upon all the actions and efforts of mind and body. Therefore, through adverse thinking almost any undesirable condition may be produced while almost any condition of worth and value can be produced through wholesome thinking. Certain processes of thought will lead to sickness, others to poverty, while processes of thought that are entirely different from these will lead to h e a l t h, p o w e r a n d prosperity. Through chaotic thinking one can bring about years of trouble and misfortune, while through a properly arranged system of thinking one can determine his own future for years and years in advance.

Everything that happens to a man is the result of something that he has done or fails to do. But since both actions and inactions come from corresponding states of mind he can make almost anything happen that he likes when he learns to regulate his thinking. This may seem to be a very strong statement, but the more perfectly we understand the relation of mental action to physical and personal action the more convinced we become that this statement is absolutely true.

When we study the laws of nature we find that certain results invariably follow certain uses of those laws; and that other results follow the misuse of those laws. We find that a misused law can finally carry you to the lowest depths, and that a law that is perfectly understood and properly applied can carry you to the greatest heights. In the use of natural law, however, we are at liberty to change our mind at any time; that is, when we find ourselves going down we can turn about and go the other way; though the fact remains that if we continue the down grade we will finally reach the lowest depths. The same is true when we find ourselves advancing; we may become negligent and fall back, but the law in question can carry us on higher and higher without end if we choose to go. The laws that govern thinking are just as absolute as the well known laws of nature and will serve man just as faithfully after he has begun to apply them with understanding.

When we understand the laws of thought and think accordingly, we have begun what may properly be termed scientific thinking; that is, we have begun designed thinking; thinking with a purpose in view; thinking in accordance with exact ~~scientific~~ system; and thinking for results. When we think in this manner we think according to those laws of thought that are required in order to produce the results we have in view; therefore all the forces of mind will be directed to produce those very results. In this connection we should remember that every mental process produces its own results in the human system; therefore we can secure any result desired when we place in action the necessary mental process.

You never think scientifically unless you think for a purpose; it is therefore purposeless thinking that you must avoid. And all purposeless thinking is wrong. Every process of thought that works at random is wrong because it leads to waste, destruction and retarded growth. For this reason all thoughts that we may create at any time that have no special purpose in view are wrong thoughts and are detrimental to the welfare of the individual. But here we must remember that wrong thought is not simply thought that has base motives; it is also thought that has no motives. A right thought always has a definite motive with some higher goal in view. In fact, to be right a thought must have a motive, and that motive must be constructive; that is, it must aim to build, and to build for something worth while. Wrong thought, however, is scattering and destructive and retards growth. This is the real difference between thought that is wrong and thought that is right. The same is true with other things. Everything in life that retards growth is wrong. Everything that promotes growth is right. If we are in doubt as to whether any particular thing is right or wrong we can readily discover where it belongs if we apply this principle; that is, if it promotes growth it is right, while if it retards growth it is wrong. We shall find that all true systems of ethics or morals will be found to harmonize perfectly with this idea.

The purpose of life is continuous advancement and all the laws of life are created for the promotion of advancement in all things and at all times. Therefore, to retard growth is to violate the laws of life while to promote growth is to properly employ those laws of life. When we go with the laws of life we move forward, but when we go against those laws we begin a life of retrogression. According to this principle nothing is wrong unless it retards growth and nothing can be right unless it promotes growth, because nothing can be wrong unless it is against the laws of life and nothing can be right unless it is in harmony with the laws of life. And the laws of life demand continuous advancement.

Since our object is advancement and progress in every way, and since thinking is the key to all results, it is evident that all thinking must be established upon the principle of continuous advancement. For this reason all thinking that in any way retards growth in any part of the human system must be discontinued, and all thinking must be so arranged or rearranged that it will tend to promote growth and advancement in every phase of human life. In other words, all thinking must be designed, and designed according to the laws that underlie the purpose we have in view. To apply this principle we should never think unless we have a purpose that we wish to promote through that thinking. Before we begin any process of thought we should determine clearly what we wish to promote at the time, and we should then employ that process of thinking through which the purpose in view may be promoted to the best advantage. /In this manner every action of mind will become constructive and will build up something that we wish to have constructed.| Neither time nor mental energy will be thrown away by aimlessness, and no chaotic states of mind will exist for a moment. All our mental processes will be arranged according to such a system of action as can promote progress, and all the various forces of mind will work together in the creation of that which we wish to realize and possess.

'To think according to the laws of growth and to think for a definite purpose—this is the foundation of scientific thinking.। This is the principle upon which to act when thinking for results, and whoever resolves to think in this manner only will soon find remarkable changes for the better taking place in every department of his life.

In training the mind to think according to the exact science of right thought, to think according to system, to think for a definite purpose and to think for results, there are four essentials that will be required and we shall proceed to give these essentials our best attention in their proper order. The first essential is to provide what may be termed the mental attitude of normal states of consciousness for all our thinking; that is, to promote only right states of mind whatever the process of thought may be, because such states are always wholesome and are invariably conducive to mental development. In addition, such states tend to hold the various energies of the mind in a working attitude which is highly important when our purpose is to work for results.

To train the mind to think only in the right states of mind we must learn to distinguish between right and wrong mental states, though this is a matter that becomes very simple when we understand that the difference between right and wrong states of mind is found in this, that the former tends to relate the mind properly to the laws, the principles and the powers of life, while the latter tends to prevent that relationship. When we are at variance with our sphere of existence or out of harmony with the world in which we think and live we can accomplish nothing, but when we are in harmony with that world we place ourselves in a position where we can accomplish practically anything if we learn the full use of all the powers we possess. Therefore, if we wish to accomplish what we have in view we must work with those laws and principles of life that govern the sphere in which our work is to be done. But wrong mental states will prevent us from working with the laws of life while right mental states have a tendency to bring us more perfectly into harmony with those laws. Wrong mental states are wrong simply because they prevent this necessary relationship, and they are wrong for no other reason. The first problem before us therefore is to distinguish between the two states of mind, to eliminate the wrong and to cultivate the right. But to distinguish between the two is not difficult when we know that right states of mind always produce harmony between ourselves and those powers in life that we must use in order to realize our purpose in life, and that wrong states of mind always take us away from everything that has quality, superiority and worth, or that can serve us in realizing the greater and the better. However, that we may all understand what mental states to cultivate in order to make our thinking more scientific, more exact, more effective and more conducive to the production of the results we desire, we shall proceed to give a brief description of the most important of these states, or what may be termed the normal and the true state of consciousness.

MONG the right states of mind the attitude of peace naturally comes first because at the foundation of all true action we find a state of deep calm. No growth is possible in confusion nor can we enjoy the steps already taken while strife and disturbance prevail. But if we find that we are not in a perfectly peaceful attitude the matter cannot be remedied through a strenuous effort to secure peace. Peace of mind comes most quickly when we do not try to be peaceful, but simply permit ourselves to be normal. To relax mind and body at frequent intervals will also aid remarkably, but the most important of all is the attainment of the consciousness of peace.

There is a state within us where all is still, and as nearly all of us have been conscious of this state at different times we know that it actually exists. To cultivate the consciousness of this state is the real secret of attaining a permanent mental state of peace. When we become conscious of that state we enter what may be termed the permanent condition of peace and thereby realize the peace that passeth understanding; and when we are in that state of peace we know why it does pass understanding.

A further proof of this idea is found in the fact that the center of all action is absolutely still, and that from this center all action proceeds. In like manner there is an absolutely still center in your own mind, and you can become conscious of that center by turning your attention gently and frequently upon the serene within. This should be done several times a day and no matter how peaceful we may feel we should daily seek a still finer realization of this consciousness of peace. The result will be more power because peace conserves energy. The mind will be kept in the necessary attitude for growth and you will avoid all such ills and failures as originate in mental confusion. According to the law that we always become in the without as we feel in the within you will naturally become more and more conscious of peacefulness in your personality as you become more conscious of the calm that is within you. In other words, the same stillness that you feel within yourself when in the consciousness of peace, will unfold itself through your entire system and you will become peaceful in every part of mind and body.

Closely related to the attitude of peace we have that of poise, and this is an attitude that is simply indispensable. The attainment of peace tends to conserve and accumulate energy while the attainment of poise tends to hold that energy in such a way that not a particle is lost. Peace is a restful attitude while poise is a working attitude. In peace you feel absolutely still. In poise you feel and hold the mighty power within you ready for action.

The well poised mind is not only charged with enormous energies, but can also retain those energies in any part of the system and can direct them towards any effort desired. The poised mind combines calmness with power. Through the attitude of calmness it retains its touch with the depths within and is thus constantly supplied with added life and power. Through the attitude of strength it relates itself to the world of action and thus becomes able to go forth and do things. The attitude of poise, however, is not well developed in the average person as the art of being peaceful and powerful at the same time is an art that has received but little attention; but it is something that is extremely important and no one who desires to learn to think and act for results can afford to neglect this high art for a moment.

To proceed with the development of poise we should work, act, think and live in the consciousness of peace and in the consciousness of power; that is, we should aim to combine peace and power in everything that we feel or do. Here we should remember two great truths; that is, that unlimited power is latent within us and that at the depth of our being everything is perfectly still. When you realize these great truths you will feel more and more that enormous energies are alive in your being, but you will find that they never force themselves into any particular line of action, and that they never run over on the surface. On the other hand, you will find that you can hold those energies in perfect repose or turn them into your work just as you wish. When you have poise therefore all those energies will also have poise. They will be as you are because they are your creations.

The effect of poise upon thinking is very great because the attitude of poise is the one essential attitude through which constructive work of mind or thought can be promoted. The object of exact scientific thinking is to bring about the results we have in view, but results follow only the true application of power, and power cannot be applied constructively unless it acts through the state of peace. We therefore understand why poise, the action of power in peace, is indispensable to every mode of thinking that aims to produce results.

Another mental state of extreme value is that of harmony; and as there is only a step from peace and poise to harmony we may readily acquire the latter when we have acquired the former. In the attitude of peace the mind finds its true self and its own supreme power. Through the attitude of poise this power is brought forth into action and is held in its true spheres of action, but it is only through harmony that this power can act properly upon things or in connection with things. Nothing comes from the application of power unless it acts directly upon something, but it cannot act upon anything with the assurance of results unless there is harmony between the power that acts and the thing acted upon. No action should be attempted therefore until harmony is secured between the two factors involved. In this connection we find that thousands of well meant actions lead to confusion, sickness and failure because no attention was given to the attainment of harmony. But the importance of attaining harmony before undertaking anything is realized when we learn that the real purpose of harmony is to bring the two factors concerned into that perfect relationship where they can work together for the promotion of the object in view.

To secure harmony it may be necessary for both factors to change their present positions. They may have to meet each other half way, but there can be no objection to this. Our object in life is not to stand where we are, but to do something; and if we can do something of value by changing our present position, that is the very thing we should do. In fact, we can even return with advantage tó positions that we imagine have been outgrown if something of value can be accomplished by such a move. The one thing to consider, however, is the result. Any movement that leads to results is a movement in the right direction.

Harmony is not cultivated by isolation nor exclusiveness. There are many minds who think they are in perfect harmony when they are alone, but they are not. They are simply at rest and the sensation is somewhat similar to certain states of harmony. We are in harmony only when we are properly related to some one else or something else. There must be at least two factors before there can be harmony and those two factors must be properly related.

The best way to cultivate the mental state of harmony is to adapt yourself consciously to everything and everybody

that you meet. Never resist or antago-
nize anything nor hold yourself aloof
from any body. Wherever you are aim
to look for the agreeable side of things
and try to act with everything while in
that attitude. After a while you will find
it an easy matter to meet all things and
all persons in their world, and when you
can do this you can unite with them in se-
curing results that neither side could have
secured alone.

To secure results two or more factors
must work together, but they cannot
work together constructively unless they
are in harmony; that is, unless they are
perfectly related to each other. To be in
harmony, however, does not mean simply
to be on good terms. You may be on
good terms with everybody and not be in
harmony with anybody. We are in har-
mony with persons and things when the
two factors or sides concerned can actu-
ally work together for the promotion of
some actual purpose. In the mental
world this law is very easily discerned
and its operations found to be exact. You
may have a fine mind, but if the different
parts of your mind do not harmonize and

wor toget er you wi accomp ish but little, and there are thousands of brilliant minds in this very condition. Then we find minds with simply a fair amount of ability who accomplish a great deal, and the reason is that the different parts of such minds are in harmony working together according to the laws of constructive action. And here we should remember that wherever two or more factors actually work together desirable results will positively follow. To agree with your adversary has the same significance. There is a certain side of every form of adversity to which you can adapt yourself. Look for that side and try to relate yourself harmoniously and constructively to the power of that side. You will avoid much trouble thereby and bring to pass scores of good things that otherwise would not have been realized.

To harmonize with the adverse does not mean that you are to follow or imitate the adverse. At all times we should be ourselves. We should change nothing in our own individuality, but should aim primarily to adapt the actions of our individuality, whether physical or mental, to those things with which we may be associated. Under all adverse circumstances we should remember that vice is virtue gone wrong and that the power in the one is the same as the power in the other; the good misdirected, that is all. But you are not to harmonize with the misdirection. You are to harmonize with the power that is back of the action and try to use that power for some valued purpose. Here we find a subject upon which volumes could be written, but the real secret that underlies it all is simple. Adapt yourself to everything and everybody with a view of securing united action for greater good. You will thus continue in perfect harmony, and you will cause every action that may result from your efforts to work directly for the production of the results you have in view.

HE three states of mind mentioned in the previous chapter will naturally lead us to a place where results can be secured, but how great these results are to be will depend upon the loftiness of our aim. Therefore a mental state will be required that will constantly center attention upon the high places of attainment, and such a state we find in aspiration. But here we must know the difference between aspiration and ambition especially when they act separately. When ambition acts aside from aspiration the aim of the mind will be to promote the personal self by calling into action only those powers that are now active in the personal self. Such an action, however, tends to separate the personality from the greater powers within which will finally produce a condition of personal inferiority. We have seen this fact illustrated so frequently that it has become proverbial to say that personal am-

bition when in full control of the mind invariably leads to personal downfall.

It is a well known fact that no mind that is simply ambitious can ever become great, and the reason is that personal ambition prevents mind and consciousness from ascending into those superior states of thought and power which alone can make greatness possible. This ascension of mind and consciousness, however, invariably takes place through the attitude of aspiration, and therefore the force of ambition should always be inspired by the spirit of aspiration. Both are necessary and they must combine perfectly in every case if results worth while are to be realized.

The attitude of aspiration causes the mind to think of the marvels that lie beyond present attainment and thereby inspires the creation of great thoughts which is vastly important. There must be great thoughts before the mind can become great, and the mind must become great before great results can be secured.

Aspiration concentrates attention upon superiority always and therefore elevates all the qualities of the mind into that state. This being true every effort in life should be directed towards those possibilities that lie beyond the present attainment if we wish to cultivate and strengthen the attitude of aspiration. When we are simply ambitious we proceed as we are and seek to make a mark for ourselves with what power we already possess; but when we are alive with the spirit of aspiration we seek to make our selves larger, more powerful and far superior to what we are now, knowing that a great light cannot be hid, and that anyone with great power must invariably reach the goal he has in view. The ambitious mind seeks to make a small light shine far beyond its capacity, and through this effort finally wears itself out. The aspiring mind, however, seeks to make the light larger and larger, knowing that the larger the light becomes the further it will shine, and that no strenuous efforts will be required to push its powerful rays into effectiveness. But when the attitude of aspiration looks beyond the personal self it does not necessarily look outside of the self. The purpose of aspiration is to enter into the possession of the marvels of the great within because what is found in the within will be expressed in the without. Therefore, when we constantly rise above the personal self we perpetually enlarge the personal self, thus gaining the capacity to accomplish more and more until we finally accomplish practically everything we have in view. The attitude of aspiration therefore should never leave the mind for a moment; but we should on the contrary keep the mental eye single upon the boundless possibilities that are within us and deeply desire with heart and soul a greater and a greater realization of those possibilities in practical life.

The attitude of contentment may truthfully be said to be the twin sister of aspiration and its important function is to prevent aspiration from losing sight of what has already been gained. When contentment is absent the present seems more or less barren, and when aspiration is absent the present seems sufficient. But the present is never barren nor is it ever sufficient. The present is rich with many things of extreme value if we only train ourselves to see them. These things, however, are not sufficient to the advancing soul. Greater things are at hand and it is our privilege to press on through the realization of those greater things. We must therefore conclude that the true attitude of mind in this connection is to be content with things as they now are, and at the same time reach out constantly for greater things.

When contentment is absent the present is not fully utilized and we cannot attain the greater things until we have fully employed what has already been received. When aspiration is absent the present is used over and over again like the air in a closed room, and the result must be mental stagnation to be followed by failure and final extinction. When we look at this subject from another point of view we find that the mind that is not contented cannot be developed; nor can such a mind make the best use of the powers it may now possess. Every moment therefore should be filled with contentment and perfect satisfaction, but every moment should also be filled with a strong desire for still greater attainments and achievements. In such a state where contentment and aspiration are combined we shall find life to be a continual feast, each course being more delicious than the one preceding. We shall also find such a life to be the path to perpetual growth and continuous joy.

To cultivate the state of contentment we should live in the conviction that all things are working together for good, and that what is best for us now is coming to us now. The truth is that if we are trying to make all things work together for good, and live in the faith that we can, we actually will so order things in our life that all things will work together for good. And what comes to us every day will be the very best for us that day. When we live, think and act in this manner we shall soon find that the best is daily coming to us, and that the best of each day is better than that of the day preceding. The result will be perfect contentment, and the placing of life in that position where it can receive in the great eternal now all that the great eternal now has to give. In brief, when we so live that we permit the present moment to be filled with all the richness that it can hold, then we shall have the contented mind and the ever-growing mind, the mind that is proverbially described as a continuous feast.

The attitude of gratitude is closely related to that of contentment and is one of the greatest of all mental states; and the reason why is found in the fact that no mind can be right nor think constructively unless it is filled with the spirit of gratitude. The fact is that new life is coming to us every day and with it new opportunities. Every moment therefore is richer than the one before; but if this coming of new life and new opportunities does not add to the richness and value of our own personal life there is a lack of gratitude. And the explanation is that where gratitude is lacking the mind is more or less closed to the many good things that are coming our way. The grateful mind, however, is always an open mind, open to the newer, the higher and the better, and therefore invariably coming into possession of more and more of those things.

The entire race is moving forward with the stream of continuous advancement;

better things therefore are daily coming into the life of each individual. If he does not receive them the reason is that his mind is more or less closed on account of the lack of gratitude. For let us remember in this connection that the mind simply must be grateful for everything in order to be open to the reception of new things and better things. We simply cannot receive better things unless we are truly grateful for that which we already possess. This is the law in this matter, and it is a law that will bear the most rigid analysis. To give thanks therefore with the whole heart for everything that comes into life, and to express constant and whole souled gratitude to all the world for everything that is good in the world—this is the secret through which we may open the mind to the great cosmic influx; that influx that is bringing into the life of every individual the richness and the power that complete life has in store for every individual.

But in order to be grateful in the best and most perfect manner we must have appreciation. We must be able to see the real worth of that which comes into life before we can express the fullness and the spirit of the grateful heart. The attitude of appreciation is also valuable in another direction. When we appreciate worth we always gain a higher consciousness of worth and thereby make our own minds more worthy.

To cultivate the mental state of appreciation we should eliminate all tendency to fault finding, criticism and the like, and we should make a special effort to see the worthy qualities in everything and everybody with which we come in contact. The result of such a practice will not only be a better appreciation, with a deeper insight into the superior qualities of life, but also the building of a more wholesome mind. Realizing the value of appreciation we should, whenever we discover a lack of appreciation in ourselves, proceed at once to remove the cause. We shall not hesitate in doing this when we find that a lack of appreciation also tends to give the mind a false view of things thereby preventing the acquisition of the best that life has in store.

The appreciative mind has a natural tendency to look upon the better side of things, but this tendency becomes complete only when the optimistic attitude is added. To be optimistic, however, does not mean to think that black is white or that everything everywhere is all right. The true optimist can also see the flaws and the imperfections in life, but he gives direct attention to the good side, the better side and the strong side. And having this larger view he always knows that the strong side is much larger and far superior to the weak side. He never becomes discouraged therefore because he knows that failure and wrong are only temporary, and that the right finally wins every time. In addition, he knows that he can aid the right to such an extent that the victory can be gained now.

The pessimist lives in the false and does not see things as they are. His conclusions are therefore worthless. For this reason we should never pay any attention to the words of the pessimist as we shall be misled in every instance if we do. Instead we should listen to the prophecy of the optimist, and then put all our ability and all our faith into the possibilities of that prophecy thereby making it come true, proceeding of course in the conviction that we can. The value of the optimistic attitude in scientific thinking therefore is very great; because to think correctly on any subject the mind must have the mountain top view, and we must think correctly if we wish to think for results.

Though the optimist may live on the sunny side, still the full value of life's sunshine cannot be gained until we add the attitude of constant cheerfulness. To be cheerful, bright, happy and joyous is absolutely necessary if we wish to think scientifically, think constructively and think for results. When we proceed to think for results we think for a purpose. We employ correctly the constructive mental processes so that we may work ourselves up to the goal in view. Growth and development therefore must take place all along the line of action, but no mental growth can take place without mental sunshine. Accordingly, we should resolve to be happy no matter what may transpire. We cannot afford to be otherwise. Sunshine will melt the most massive iceberg if the rays are direct and the clouds are kept away; and it is the same in daily life. No matter how cold, disagreeable and uncongenial your present environment may be, plenty of mental sunshine can change it all.

It pays to be happy. Cheerfulness is a most profitable investment and there are no riches that are greater than constant joy. This attitude is not for the few or for occasional moments because all the sunny states of mind can be made permanent in a short time by a very simple process. Make it a practice to go to sleep every night with cheerfulness on your mind and with a feeling of joy in every atom of your being. Through this practice you will carry the cheerful idea into the subconscious, and gradually the joyous state will become an established state in the subconscious mind. The result will be that the subconscious will express cheerfulness and wholesomeness at all times, and it will become second nature for you to have a sweet disposition, a sunny frame of mind and an attitude of perpetual joy. This method may seem to be too simple to be of value, but the simplest methods are usually the best. And anyone can prove through a few weeks of trial that this method will produce the desired results, and will through more continuous practice actually transform mind and disposition to such an extent that the mind will henceforth live in constant mental sunshine. And there are few things that are more important than this if we wish to train the mind to act and work in those attitudes that are necessary in order that we may proceed successfully in thinking for results.

HE attitude of kindness is one of the greatest among the right states of mind. Therefore to be kind to everybody and to feel kindly towards the whole of creation, this must be the attitude if the right use of mind and thought is to prevail. Kindness enlarges the inner consciousness thus promoting the enlargement and the expression of life. And it also creates the tendency to give one's best and there is nothing that brings forth the greater life and power within us so quickly and so completely as the giving of one's best in all things and at all times.

Both the soul and the mind, with all their powers and possibilities, tend to unfold themselves through the actions of the strong whole souled attitude of kindness. In fact, no one can begin to unfold his larger life and receive the greater richness from within until he begins to give, through the attitude of kindness, all that which he already has in his personality. And the more one gives of the richness of one's own life, ability and power, the more he will receive from the limitless realms of the within. This is a law that no one, not even the most materialistic, can afford to ignore. But giving is not giving unless it comes from the heart, and it must invariably be an act of expression for some great purpose. Your expressions, either of thought or action, will not open the way for inner unfoldment unless you give richly through a fuller and larger expression, and in all such expressions you must feel kindly. The attitude of kindness is therefore indispensable to growth, mental unfoldment and constructive thinking.

The attitude of sympathy always acts in close connection with kindness, and though it is a most important state of mind it is also a much abused state. There are few people who sympathize correctly and there is possibly nothing that interferes with correct thinking as does misdirected sympathy. When we sympathize with anyone we enter into a certain unity of that one's mind and we almost invariably imitate to a degree the mind that we unite with in this way. Two minds with but a single thought will imitate each other in nearly everything and will actually grow to look alike. It is therefore very important to know with what we should sympathize. When you sympathize with a person in distress you will think the thought of distress at the time, and will reproduce in a measure the same state in your own mind, and possibly in your own life and personality. Many a person has failed in life because he has sympathized too much with the weak side and inferior side of those who have had misfortune. When you sympathize with a person that is sick your mind will create within itself a similar condition of disease, and this expression will express itself in your own body, a fact to which thousands can testify. We realize again therefore that it will not do to sympathize with anything and everything that may arouse our sympathy.

Why does it hurt to see a friend punished? Why do we usually feel bad when those of whom we think a great deal feel bad? Why is there a tendency of most minds to think and feel like the prevailing thought in their community? Why does a mob lose its head, so to speak, and proceed to think, feel and act precisely like the leader? Why do scores of incidents of a similar nature take place in our midst constantly? Sympathetic imitation explains such phenomena. And the law that underlies this phenomena is a law that we must understand thoroughly if we wish to master our own thinking and our actions wherever those actions may be expressed. When you sympathize with weakness you are liable to become weak. When you sympathize with disease you are liable to get the same symptoms and frequently the very disease itself. When you sympathize with the wrong you are liable to think that same wrong and possibly act it out in your own life. These are facts with which we are all familiar. It is therefore a subject of extreme importance. The law that governs sympathy is this, that you enter into mental unity in a measure with everything with which you sympathize, and that whatever you enter into mental unity with you tend to imitate and produce in yourself to a degree. Understanding this law we realize that we cannot afford to sympathize with everything, but on the contrary find it absolutely necessary to make a careful selection of those things with which we may sympathize.

When you sympathize with a person who is in trouble do not think of the trouble or the pain or the weakness, but think of that something within him that is superior to all pain and that can annihilate all the trouble in existence. Then remember the great statement that "he that is within you is greater than he that is in the world." Make it a practice never to sympathize with the inferior side, but only with the superior side. But this will not make you cold and indifferent as many suppose, for it is impossible for you to become mentally cold while being in touch with the very life of the soul itself which must be the very essence of tenderness, kindness and love. In applying this principle we find that the more perfectly you sympathize with the higher, the finer and the stronger side of man the more love you feel, the more tenderness you express and the more helpful you become in all of your efforts. Nothing is lost, therefore, but much is gained by training the mind to sympathize only with the true side of human life.

The man who is sick and in trouble does not want more tears. He has had enough of them. What he wants and what he needs is that sympathy that can banish all tears and that can reveal the way to emancipation, power and joy. This being true we must try to banish completely every form of morbid sympathy. It hurts everybody. It perpetuates weakness and keeps the mind in bondage to inferior imitations. In applying this higher form of sympathy do not tell the unfortunate that you are sorry. Tell them how to get rid of their sorrow. Then do something substantial to speed them on the way. This is sympathy that is worthy of the name.

Right thinking cannot be promoted so long as we sympathize in the old fashioned way. We cannot think constructively so long as we permit the mind to imitate the wrong, the weak, the inferior and the destructive. Here, however, we find a problem that we must solve because it is natural for the mind to imitate to a certain degree. We should therefore give the mind something to imitate that has quality and superiority. In brief, we should train the mind to imitate the strong, the worthy, the superior and the ideal, and thus cause all mental actions to produce the strong, the worthy, the superior and the ideal in ourselves. For the mind invariably tends to create that which we think of the most.

The true attitude of sympathy will be promoted to a very great extent if we train ourselves to live in the upper story or rather the idealistic state of mind. There are two planes upon which the mind can dwell and they are usually called the idealistic and the materialistic. The ideal plane is the upper plane while the materialistic is the lower. In the idealistic all the tendencies of the mind move towards the qualities of superiority and worth; all the desires are for the higher and the better; all thoughts are created after the likeness of our higher conceptions of the perfect, the true and the superior. To live in such an attitude is to be an idealist and this is the meaning of idealism. An idealistic mind therefore is a mind that is constantly ascending, and thus taking a larger view and a more beautiful view every day of the richness and splendor of real existence.

In the materialistic attitude all the tendencies of mind move toward the superficial, the inferior and the imperfect. In this attitude we usually think according to those false conceptions of things that have been handed down by the race, and all our desires are concerned principally with satisfying the needs of the body. The materialistic mind is the descending mind, the mind that is losing ground gradually, and that is daily being overcome more and more by its own perverted and materialistic thought habits. But to live in the upper story is to keep the mind concentrated upon the great possibilities that are latent within us and to desire with the whole heart the daily realization of more and more of the wonders that are in store for those who are steadily pressing on towards greater things. In the upper story we live with greatness. In the lower story we live with mistakes and inferiority. In the upper story we see that man is daily unfolding the greatness of the super-man. In the lower story we see only the depravity or weakness of error and sin. In the lower story we are in partial or complete darkness. In the upper story we are in the full light. It is therefore easily understood why the mind must dwell in the upper story before right thinking can begin.

After beginning to live in the upper story the consciousness of superiority and supremacy will naturally appear, and these two states should be thoroughly developed. We should all train ourselves to feel that we are superior beings; not superior to others because we are all superior, but superior to everything that pertains to personal existence; superior to ills, pains, weaknesses, mistakes and failures; and superior to everything that is imperfect or undeveloped. Here we should remember that the consciousness of superiority does not produce vanity or egotism. When a person has really become conscious of the superiority of his true being he is above all small and questionable states of mind.

When you are superior you do not have to make any display of the matter to prove it. It will show in your life and in your work, and actions speak more eloquently than words. The principal reason why the attitude of superiority is so important is because it unites the mind with everything in your life and your thought that has quality, and thereby gives everything in your mind and personality the stamp of greater worth. And it is a well known fact that whenever we enrich our thought, or any expression of thought, we tend to enrich everything in our life and those things that we produce through our work.

The attitude of supremacy should refer to your own being only. To rule supremely in your own domain and not interfere with the domain of any one else —this is the true purpose of self-supremacy. And the value of self-supremacy is realized not only in its power to give the individual self-mastery, but also in the fact that when the mind feels that it is superior it can more easily think its own thoughts and thereby prevent the practice of imitating false actions or ideas. It must therefore be quite evident that this state is absolutely necessary to scientific thinking and to the art of thinking for results.

The mind that recognizes its own supremacy is a strong mind and will therefore seek to extend its power wherever the enlargement of life can be promoted, but to accomplish this the mind must be positive; that is, every action of the mind should be filled, so to speak, with a thought current that tends to press on and on to the goal in view The positive mind, however, does not force its way, but wins because it is strong, and every mind becomes strong when constantly filled with thoughts that are positive and determined. To the attitude of positiveness we should add those of push and perseverance because these two attitudes tend to promote the increase of the results that are already being gained; and there is nothing that succeeds like that which is constantly pressing on to greater success.

When we proceed to think for results

we are invariably imbued with the spirit of advancement. Therefore to increase the power of this spirit the mind should cultivate the persevering attitude and should feel a strong desire to push forward into the ever enlarging realms of perpetual growth. But in this connection we must not forget courage and patience, nor the progressive attitude. It has been well said that we all could accomplish far more if we would only attempt more, but in the majority courage generally fails when in the presence of great undertakings. This, however, we cannot afford to permit. To the attitude of courage we should add the mental states of self-reliance and self-confidence and still greater gain will be realized. In fact, these two states are of such value that their importance cannot be described in words. They are not sufficiently developed in the average person, however, because he depends too much upon environments, opportunities and associates, and not enough upon himself. The great soul depends upon nothing exterior to himself. Such a soul makes opportunities to order and changes environments to comply with requirements. Such a soul turns adversity into a willing servant and makes every obstacle a new path to greater achievement. But no soul can become a great soul until faith in its own power has become unbounded.

The strong, positive mind may at times go beyond its own domain and may some times act in realms where it has no legal right, but this can be prevented through the attitude of non-resistance, another most important attitude in the art of constructive thinking. The attitude of resistance is always destructive and therefore interferes with the real purpose of right thinking. But it is not necessary to resist anything. That which is inferior will disappear when we produce the superior and not until then. It is therefore a waste of time and energy to try to remove wrong through resistance. The proper course to pursue is to build up the right and the wrong will disappear of itself. In this connection, however, it may seem to be difficult to continue in a non-resisting attitude when we are constantly in the presence of adverse conditions. But here we should remember that the mind that is constantly creating the larger and the better will hardly be aware of the imperfect in his life because the imperfect is constantly passing away with the ceaseless coming and upbuilding of the more perfect. Our purpose should be never to resist evil; though we should not on the other hand fold our arms and let things be as they are. While we are turning away from lesser things we should concentrate our whole attention upon the building up of the greater. This is a method that will give perfect freedom and continuous advancement to us all.

To the practice of non-resistance we should add forgiveness. Forgive everybody, even yourself. To condemn anything or anybody is a misuse of the mind. So long as we condemn the wrong the mind is forcefully directed towards the wrong. The mental picture of wrong becomes more deeply stamped upon the subconscious, and more thoughts and mental states will be created in the likeness of those impressions or pictures. These impressions will reproduce themselves in us and this is how we tend to create in ourselves what we condemn in others. The reverse of this principle is also true; that is, that we tend to create and build up in ourselves the good that we commend and appreciate in others.

To promote the cultivation of forgiveness we should become conscious of real purity, and the reason for this is readily understood when we remember the statement about the eye that is too pure to behold iniquity. Why the pure eye does not see evil is a subject too large to be discussed here. But we shall find that the more perfectly we develop the consciousness of purity the smaller and more insignificant evil becomes to us, and the easier it becomes to forgive everybody for everything. In the attitude of mental purity we look upon the mistakes of the world in the same way as we look upon the false notes that the child makes while learning to play. We want those false notes corrected, but we do not call them bad. We know that the child will learn to play perfectly later on, not by being punished or scolded, but by being taught thoroughly and persistently. It is the same with the mistakes of the human race, and those mistakes should be dealt with in the same manner.

One of the very important states of the mind is that of justice, or the consciousness of justice, and it is most necessary that we cultivate the habit of being just even in minute details. The just mind can readily direct its processes of thought and creation into those channels of action that are in harmony with the laws of life, while the mind that is not just will misdirect many of those processes and thereby produce all kinds of detrimental conditions of mind and body. In a state of justice everybody has his own. Therefore to be just is to so act that you never deprive anyone of his own nor fail to render to anyone that which is his own. To know what really belongs to you and what really belongs to others, however, may at first sight seem to be a difficult problem, but we cannot solve it by looking at external possessions. We become just by developing the consciousness of justice and not by measuring this to one and that to the other. To execute justice in the world, or in connection with any of our own actions, we must realize justice in our own soul because effects do not precede causes. And if all moral teachers in the world would cease their criticisms of powers and systems and give their entire attention to the development of the consciousness of justice in the mind of the race, we should soon have an order of things which would be absolutely just to all. In our own thinking, however, the attainment of this consciousness of justice is so absolutely necessary that it should be given a most prominent place in all our efforts, because it is only through the consciousness of justice that all misdirection of thought and energy can be prevented.

There are three additional states of mind required to make this study complete, and these are refinement, receptivity and faith. But we need not take the time to give them special attention as we all understand their nature and importance. Faith and receptivity have special functions to perform in all kinds of mental actions and development, and the advancing process of the mind must of necessity be a refining process; otherwise growth would be an impossibility. The purpose of scientific thinking therefore cannot be promoted unless the entire system is permeated with the consciousness of refinement. And to attain this consciousness we should picture before us the most refined state of the ideal that we can possibly conceive, and keep this picture before us constantly with the deep desire to make it real.

The above is a brief analysis of the most important of the right mental states —those states that are needed to place the mind in that state of action that is absolutely necessary if we wish to think for results. We are now ready therefore to proceed with the real process of thinking.

VERY normal person has a definite goal that he expects to reach; some purpose for which he is living, thinking and working; one or more objects that he is trying to gain possession of. But how to realize this ambition is the problem, and though he hopes to find the solution in some way, that way is not always as clear as he should wish it to be. A study of natural laws, however, both physical and metaphysical will readily reveal the secret.

When we study natural laws we find that aimless living is wasteful, deteriorating and detrimental both to the individual and to the race, and the same study reveals the fact that all the laws of nature are constructed for the promotion of progress and growth. Therefore to be natural we must move forward, and to move forward we must have a definite purpose. From this we conclude that the life with a definite purpose is the only natural life.

And as it is natural, nature must be able to provide a way by which such a life can be perfected fully and completely. In other words, there must be a solution for every problem, and this being true, he who seeks the solution will certainly find it.

Nature is dual, physical and metaphysical. What we fail to find in the one, therefore, we shall certainly find in the other; and the study of the larger metaphysics gives us the solution for the problem under consideration. This solution is based upon the discovery that thought is the one power that determines the life, the position, the circumstances and the destiny of man, and that to use that power we must learn to think for results.

Whether 'the individual is to move forward or not depends upon what he thinks. His actions, his intentions, his motives, his plans, his tendencies, his efforts—all of these play their part, but they are all the products of thinking, and therefore are invariably like the process of thinking from which they sprang. Every thought is a power in the life where it is created and will either promote or retard the purpose of that life. Every thought you think is either for you or against you. It will either push you forward or hold you down. When your own thought is against you all your actions, efforts, tendencies, plans, intentions, and everything that is produced by thought or directed by thought will also be against you; and conversely everything that you do with muscle or brain will be for you when your thought is for you. This is a fact the importance of which is certainly great. And since it has been fully demonstrated to be a fact we cannot afford to give it less than our most profound attention.

Since it is natural to have definite aims in life, in fact absolutely necessary in order to be in harmony with the purpose of life, and since it is natural to move forward, it must be natural to have only such thoughts as are for you; thoughts that can push you forward and that will be instrumental in promoting the purpose you have in view. In other words, to comply with the laws of nature, physical and metaphysical, it is necessary to think in such a way that all mental action tends to produce growth, advancement and progress. In this connection we find that nature's laws do not conflict. One law declares that the individual must move forward constantly if he would be in accord with nature, and another law declares that our thoughts will either promote or retard the forward movement. Therefore when our thinking retards our progress we violate natural law and will consequently produce conditions that are detrimental.

To discriminate between right and wrong thinking, between scientific and chaotic thinking, and all thinking is chaotic that is not scientific, becomes very simple when we define the former as being in accord with natural laws, and the latter as being at variance with natural laws. Or to be more explicit, scientific thinking is the formation of all such mental actions, mental states and mental forces as have the power to produce in our efforts what nature has given all things in the human system the power to produce. It is the intention of nature that all things shall work for perpetual advancement of all things. Therefore a thought to be in accord with nature must have the inherent impulse as well as the power to promote advancement in its sphere of action.

To be scientific is to be in accord with nature; to work physically and mentally with nature, and to carry out the fundamental intentions of nature. And since all the actions of man are produced and directed by his thinking, he cannot work with nature unless his thinking is in accord with nature, and is designed and applied with definite results in view. In brief, thinking is scientific and designed when its purpose is to produce advancement, and when it has at the same time both the power and the knowledge to carry out that purpose.

Every intelligent person tries to live in accord with natural laws, but as a rule complies only with those laws that deal with the physical side of life. He therefore cannot be in perfect accord with nature because to obey one group of laws and ignore another group will produce nothing but confusion and ultimate failure. And what is important, it is not possible to comply perfectly with physical laws unless we understand metaphysical laws. Physical actions are both produced and directed by mental action. Not a muscle can move unless the mind moves. Therefore, if the mental action is not fully in accord with natural laws it will not be possible for the consequent physical actions to be in full accord with nature. It is not difficult to understand therefore why the majority of those who have tried to live in accord with nature, and tried to apply fully the powers and possibilities of nature, have not succeeded in as large a measure as their ambitions might desire. They have tried to bring physical actions into harmony with nature while their mental actions have been more or less at variance with nature. They have tried to make their actions scientific while their thinking remained unscientific. And here we have the cause of practically all the trouble, confusion and failure in the world.

The statement that nature's fundamental intention is the perpetual advancement of all things, may be questioned when we take note of the many processes of nature that appear to be destructive, and find that those processes invariably work in harmony with natural law. But when we look beneath the surface we find that the consuming process is necessary to the refining process, and that the decomposing process is indispensable to growth. That which destroys does not tend directly to build up, but the inferior must be removed before the superior can be constructed. The force of destruction, however, can be used in many ways. It can be turned into the gross actions of the sledge that tears down the present structure. Or it can be employed through the channel of transmutation which removes the present structure, not by tearing it down, but by changing it into something better. In the grosser forms of action destruction is usually separated from construction, and may or may not be followed by the latter, but in the higher forms of action destruction and construction are one. The inferior is destroyed by being immediately transmuted into the superior. And here we should remember that everything in nature regardless of its present condition can be transformed into something higher, finer and better because every process in nature can promote advancement, being created for that purpose. Therefore to be in accord with nature man must have the same purpose. He must live, think and work for perpetual advancement, constant growth and eternal progress.

In preceding pages it has been stated that the foundation of scientific thinking consists of thinking only in the attitude of right mental states, and the principal right mental states were enumerated and defined; and in this connection it may be added that the reason why such states of mind constitute the foundation of scientific thinking is based upon the fact that wrong mental states tend to pervert and misdirect the original intention of every process of thinking, while right mental states tend to hold in position, so to speak, or properly direct the original intention of every mental process. To think scientifically and to think for results is to think with a definite object in view; that is, to so think that every thought will aid

in the realization of that object. There-
fore it cannot be scientific to originate
a mental process with a certain object in
view and then permit that process to be
misdirected, but this is what we con-
tinue to do so long as wrong mental
states are permitted to act in the mind.

A misdirected mental process always
creates thoughts and mental actions that
are foreign or adverse to the original in-
tention of that process and are in conse-
quence detrimental. Such thinking there-
fore does not only waste time and effort,
but places serious obstacles in the way of
our constructive and properly directed ef-
forts. In the average mind we find men-
tal states that are right as well as mental
states that are wrong. The one group
assists the forward movement of mind
while the other not only retards or mis-
directs, but usually acts as an obstacle as
well. This, however, we cannot afford to
permit. The proper course to take there-
fore in the very beginning is to eliminate
absolutely all mental states that are
wrong and to shun them completely in
the future. Should we be in doubt as to
what states are wrong, we need only re-

member that every mental state is wrong that has no tendency to build, and that every state is right that does have a direct upbuilding tendency. And in eliminating the wrong states of mind the simplest method is to give so much attention to the creation and the strengthening of right mental states that not a single mental action is ever permitted to create or perpetuate wrong states. In other words, there will be no power with which to produce the wrong when all the power of the mind is used in building up the right.

We may proceed, therefore, upon the principle that right mental states constitute the foundation of scientific thinking, and that the very first thing to do in learning how to think for results is to train the mind to create, entertain, and perpetuate only right mental states. When we have established this foundation we may proceed with the first story of the superstructure. To this structure there are several stories, but the first one is to give every thought you think the tendency and the power to promote your own individual purpose in life; that is, every mental action, every mental creative process and every form of thinking should be so constituted that everything that transpires in the mind will work both fully and directly for your welfare and advancement. In other words, train your mind to think only thoughts that will push your work, and every thought you think can push your work if properly constructed. But the opposite is also true. Every thought you think can interfere with your work if not properly constructed. We realize therefore the importance of discriminating between the right and the wrong even in the most insignificant of our mental attitudes, because we want everything that takes place in our system to act to our advantage.

Before you can apply scientific thinking in your own life it is necessary to make a definite decision as to what purpose you wish to live, think and work for. And in most minds this purpose will assume a three fold aspect. The first will be to succeed in your vocation; the second will be a continuous development of the leading mental qualities;

and the third will be the attainment of higher and higher states of ideal existence. To these three many may wish to add the development of one or more special talents, or the attainment of certain special objects, and these different things can easily be added without interfering with the full promotion of the general purpose. The idea is that you must clearly fix in mind what you wish to think and work for in the great eternal now. In the future, some or all of your plans may be changed, but you may do that when the future comes. While the present remains there must be something definite to work for now, and that something should receive your undivided attention. By doing justice to the present we shall be far better equipped for the opportunities of the future. In fact the very best way to prepare for the future is to be your very best in the present, and if you are your best in the present your future will certainly be better.

Whether you have a few objects or many that you wish to realize, place them properly in your mind giving each a special position before your mental vision, and then hold these objects constantly before you as the great goal for which you desire to live, think and work. Center all attention upon that goal, mentally moving m that direction every moment, and turning on the full current. No force of thought or action must go to the left or to the right. Every force you place in action in your system must aim upon that goal, and must proceed with the definite purpose of helping you reach that goal. In brief, you must actually live in every sense of the word for the purpose you have in view. That does not mean, however, that you must ignore the interest of others or become oblivious to the many phases of life that exist about you. The mind is complex and consciousness is capable of many grades of action; therefore you can in general be interested in everything that has worth. But all these other interests must be made a channel through which your fundamental purpose can be promoted, or rather an aid to the great plan for which you live, think and work. If you are a business man you need not ignore music, art or literature. The more you have of these the better for your business provided you employ them as forces of inspiration. Though it is necessary for you to concentrate your life upon your business, still you must constantly enlarge your mind, character and soul in order to insure increased success in your business. Your capacity for work and your power to improve the quality of your work must develop. And everything in life that has worth can be made to promote your own individual growth. In other words, be interested in everything that has quality and worth anywhere in life and use everything you gain through this interest for the making of your own life larger, richer and more successful.

It is not the narrow mind that succeeds. The mind that invariably realizes the greatest success is the mind that is broad, and at the same time has the power to focus the whole of its larger capacity upon the one thing that is being done now. When you constantly focus your mind upon that which you are living for and working for you are giving all your creative powers to those faculties and talents that are required in the realization' of your objects in view. It is therefore evident that the larger your mind is, both in its capacity and power the greater will be the results. It requires ability and power to do things. Therefore the more ability and the more power you can apply in any line of action the more you will accomplish and the more rapidly you will advance in that direction. For this reason we do not wish to throw away ability and power upon those things that cannot promote our present progress. We do not wish to give thought and attention to plans that are of no use to us now. We may need those plans some day, but the plans that we can use now are the only ones that have a right to our present attention.

The idea is to think that you can, to think for results and to give your life in the present to that which can use your life in the present. This is not done, however, when we permit aimless thinking. And the amount of life and ability that is thrown away in this manner is enormous. Aimless thinking has the same effect upon your capacity and ability as punching holes in the boiler has upon the capacity of the engine. But the giving of attention to foreign or temporary plans is just as wasteful. When you decide upon a plan see it through. Give your whole life to it. Turn the full force of your whole mind upon it and keep at it until you are ready for some greater plan. You will thus build yourself up and prepare yourself for a greater plan, and when such a plan arrives, which it positively will, drop everything else and give this new plan the full force of your undivided attention.

Too many minds are constantly wishing they were in some other kind of work, thus diverting their attention every few moments from the work in which they are engaged now. The result is not only poor work, but they place themselves in a position where they can never find opportunity for advancement. If you want something better to do, do your present work so well that it becomes a stepping stone to something better. It is the man who thoroughly fills his present place that is asked to come up and fill a larger place, but no man can fill his present place to full capacity unless all the life and all the power that is in him is applied directly in producing results in that place.

Since thought is a definite power, with great constructive possibilities, the more thought we give to our work the more successful we shall be in that work provided our thought is scientific, designed and constructive. This is simple. On the other hand whenever we encourage aimless thinking or wishing for something else to do we are taking power away from our work thereby decreasing results. One of the first principles in thinking for results therefore is to give your whole attention to your present work; to give all your creative power to the building up of the purpose at hand; and to cause every mental action to act in such a way that it will act with the plans and for the plans you are now seeking to push through.

HE next question that will naturally arise is that of knowing what to think about our work and the objects we have in view. Every mental state becomes the mother of ideas; every idea can produce a tendency of mind, and every tendency tends to draw mental actions in its own direction. A false conception will produce false ideas, false ideas will originate false tendencies and false tendencies will lead the mind into mistakes. To promote any purpose, however, mistakes must be avoided as far as possible. Everything must be done correctly, and whatever is done should be done better and better every time. The way we think therefore of what we are to do or the objects we have in view will directly determine the results that are to be attained.

When you think about your work as being difficult you form a wrong mental conception; for the fact is that **no** work is more difficult than we make it, and we can relate ourselves to our work in such a way that we shall always be equal to the occasion. When you think about your work as difficult you will usually approach it in the attitude of doubt and fear, and no mind can do its best while in such states. Nor can you relate yourself to your work under such conditions because the false mental tendencies that follow such false conceptions will mislead many or all of your faculties. To think of your work as being completely under your personal control is correct because the possibilities within us are unlimited and we can make ourselves equal to any occasion. From this we are not to infer, however, that we can do now whatever our personal opinions may conclude that we can do now; for such opinions are not always based upon the whole truth in the matter. But the idea is that you can succeed in that work which your best judgment has decided upon, and that you can increase your success in that line more and more for an indefinite period.

To think of your work as trivial, mean

or burdensome is wrong because such an attitude of mind will tend to make you inferior, and there is no success for you while you are on the downgrade towards inferiority. To think of your work as ordinary or trivial is to think ordinary thoughts, and as such thoughts will decrease the power of your mind they will naturally interfere with your work and therefore be directly against you in their actions. To think of your work as drudgery, or as something disagreeable that is to be gone through with is in like manner a mistake; the reason being that such thinking prevents the mind from being its best and giving expression to its best. You cannot give your heart and soul to that which you despise, and you cannot do your best in any kind of work unless you give it your whole heart and soul.

If you want to think and work for results you must love your work, and you can, though such love is not to be sentimental, but rather the feeling of intense admiration for those lines of action that you know will lead to greater things. Think therefore of your work as a channel through which you are to reach the higher places of life because that is what your work really is if you approach it in the right way and apply its possibilities on the largest scale. To find fault with what you have accomplished is wrong as it tends to turn attention upon defects and inferiority. Every mind should constantly expect to do better and should with every effort try to improve upon what was done before, but no actual or chronic fault finding must be permitted. To find fault with what you have done is to belittle yourself; in brief, to place a wet blanket, so to speak, over your hopes and aspirations. Instead, you should think of your work as very good considering your present development, but you should set your whole heart and soul upon the attainment of something far superior. Think constantly of your work as being susceptible to perpetual improvement. Then proceed to make that thought come true, and you will positively succeed.

Every mental process that you turn into your work must be constructive. Your object is progress towards the goal you have in view. Therefore, every process that you place in action whether in mind or personality must be a building process. But your desire to make those processes constructive will not alone make them so. The idea of constant enlargement must be the very soul of every thought, and the whole of your mentality must live and act in a state of expanding consciousness. In the growing mind there is an interior ever-increasing feeling of the consciousness of enlargement and expansion which we should cultivate extensively, and in this feeling every process of thinking should move. The thought that you put into your work will increase or decrease your capacity, and will consequently either promote or retard your progress. And here we should remember that the thought you put into your work is the thought you think while you work. While you work you are actually giving a part of yourself to that which you are doing, but if you are giving your life and power correctly you will receive more than you give; that is, the reaction will be greater than the action. In order to give correctly of your life and power in this manner, or rather to think correctly while at work, every mental action in expression at the time should be permeated with the spirit of expansion, improvement and advancement. In brief, you should feel that the effort you put into your work is actually developing yourself. And this is precisely what is taking place in every mind that thinks scientifically, constructively and according to a definite purpose while at work.

Your thought about the progress of your work is very important and such thought should always be that of success. If you are determined to succeed your work is already a success, and it is strictly scientific to think of it as such. When the seed is good and has been placed in good soil we can truthfully say that a good harvest will be forthcoming. In like manner, you can truthfully say that you are a success when all the elements needed to produce success have been placed in action in your own mind and personality. Too many minds, however, do not recognize success until they see the physical results and for this very reason the physical results are fre-, quently limited or of inferior worth; the reason being that the real spirit of success was absent during the actions of that process through which the physical results were being produced. But the cause of success has the same right to recognition as the effect of success, and if the cause is recognized in the beginning the effects will become much larger because the process will contain a much larger measure of the spirit of success. When we give conscious recognition to a cause we increase its power. When you have selected a work and have resolved to put your whole life into it you are already a success in that work, and it is perfectly right for you to think of yourself as a success. The cause of that success has been created; therefore that success already does exist. And by giving it faith, encouragement and mental power it will continue to grow, and will finally produce all kinds of rich harvests or tangible results in the external world.

When a powerful cause has been created the effect is inevitable, provided it is not destroyed during its process of expression. Wrong thought, however, has a tendency to destroy every constructive cause that may have been placed in action in the mind. Therefore we must think correctly, harmoniously and constructively of every process of thought or action all along the line; that is, we should give every good cause definite recognition as an individual power and give it full right of way in our world. To create a good cause and then ignore it is to deprive it of life during its infancy, but this is the very thing we do when we proceed in the belief that we may succeed some day. Say instead, and say it with all the power of mind and soul, I AM SUCCESS NOW. Every true effort is successful because it not only has the power to produce success, but is actually working out successful results; and if it is encouraged, pushed and promoted it will positively express the success desired in real life. To push or promote a true effort we should think of it as being already an individual power for success, because that is what it is, and by dealing with it as such we turn our creative powers into its sphere of action which means that the desired results will invariably follow.

The progress of anything will necessarily depend upon the methods employed. Therefore, the way we plan for greater achievements and the methods we employ in promoting our advancement, are matters of extreme importance. Every plan should be directly related to the purpose which it is intended to promote, and every method we employ should be based upon the laws required to carry it out. It is also important to increase the capacity of every new plan as much as possible. In formulating the best plans and methods, however, the laws of life should be thoroughly understood especially those laws that act in the metaphysical field because all physical action to be effective must be preceded by effective mental actions. But in addition to having the right methods, the right plans and the knowledge of constructive action, physical and mental, we must also have a powerful faith if we wish to work and think for results. When we plan for greater things and have faith in greater things we shall certainly see those greater things realized. In fact, the power of faith in the promotion of any plan or purpose is so great that no one can afford to give it otherwise than the most thorough attention. Though faith in one of its phases is what may be termed a mental attitude, an attitude with an upward look, still it is in its most important phase a positive mental force. The mental force or action of faith is always elevating, expanding and constructive. Therefore, to have faith in yourself and in your work is to cause all the powers of your mind to become elevating, expanding and constructive in all their actions. Faith always tends to build and it builds the loftier, the perfect and the more worthy. Doubt, however, retards and retreats; it is a depressing mental state that we cannot afford to entertain for a moment. But such a state can be removed at once by cultivating faith; and as we proceed to get faith we should by all means get an abundance of faith for in all efforts that aim for great results we cannot have too much faith.

It has been said that faith and science can never harmonize, because according to some they are antagonistic, and according to others they act in domains that are wholly dissimilar. But no matter what the views of the past may be on the subject the fact is that there is nothing more scientific than faith, and also that there is nothing that will aid the mind more in becoming scientific and constructive than a thorough realization, as well as expression, of the spirit of faith. The more familiar we become with real faith the more convinced we become that faith is indispensable in every effort we make, physical or mental, if the best results are to be secured. In fact, faith must be made the very soul of every thought, and the living spirit of every mental action. For this reason we realize that no greater step forward can be taken than to give faith the first place in life if our purpose in life is to think and work for results.

AN is 'as he thinks and his thoughts are invariably created in the likeness of his mental conceptions of those things of which he thinks about habitually. Therefore as man improves his mental conceptions of all things he will improve himself in the same measure. To improve these mental conceptions attention should always be concentrated upon the ideal of everything of which we think. That is, all thinking should move toward the greater, the larger and the superior. Whatever we think about we should always think about its ideal side, its larger side and its superior side. Everything has two sides, the limited or objective side and the unlimited or subjective side. When we consider only the limited objective side of those things we think about our mental conceptions will be small, superficial and materialistic. But when we consider the unlimited subjective side of those things our mental

conceptions will be larger, finer and of far superior worth.

The capacity, the power and the brilliancy of the mind depends entirely upon its mental conceptions. If the mental conceptions are formed in the likeness of the external, common or the ordinary, the mind will be inferior in every respect, and vice versa. It is therefore of the highest importance that every mental conception be as high, as perfect and as ideal as it is possible to make it. And to bring this about it is necessary to train the mind to concentrate attention upon the ideal side of everything and to think with the larger, the greater and the superior always in view.

When thinking about persons no mental conceptions should be formed of the mere external or personal side. The superior man alone should receive direct attention. To look through the person, so to speak, and view the inner possibilities, and all the worthy qualities that we know to exist back of the imperfect manifestation—this is the correct and the scientific way to think about the people we meet. When we analyze the inferior things we see about a person and permit those things to affect our minds we form inferior and detrimental conceptions in our own minds. When we think a great deal about the smallness we imagine we see in others we tend to breed smallness in ourselves. But when we think only of the larger and the better side of others we cause our minds to rise in the scale and thus gain power and understanding we never had before. In this connection the law is that when we look with deep interest for everything that is superior in others we actually develop the superior in ourselves.

When we think of the body we should not think of it as common flesh as the majority do, because the physical form will tend to express the crude and the common when we think of it in that way. When your mental actions are low, crude and coarse your body will have an ordinary earth-earthy appearance, but when those actions are highly refined your body will express a more refined appearance to correspond. All such actions constitute, or are produced by, the thoughts we think. Therefore all our mental actions are as crude or as fine as our thoughts themselves. To be scientific in this, however, we should think of the body as a great temple with millions of apartments, each one furnished most gorgeously with nature's own wealth and beauty, and this is what the body really is. Every cell of the body when viewed under a microscope is like a crystal palace, and the body is composed of millions of such. We should always think of the body as a divinely formed structure, as an ideal creation, and we should mentally view its perfect elements, its forces and laws in this manner as they perform their daily miracles. We should think of the body as it is in its true inner self, as it is in its fine and delicate structures and we should not think of those imperfections in its appearance which our own crude mental actions have produced; for when we form in mind the highest conception possible of the ideal physical form we will not only cause the body to grow more beautiful every year, but we will also enrich the mind with thoughts of high and superior worth.

When we think of the mind we should

not think of its flaws or undeveloped states, but try to realize how great and wonderful the mind really is, and then hold attention upon our highest conception of true greatness. When all our mental activities move towards this lofty idea of a brilliant and prodigious mind we shall steadily develop our own mind up to that superior state; for according to a well known metaphysical law we mentally move towards the ideals we persistently hold in mind. Therefore by directing our attention upon the greater side of the mind we shall actually arise into mental greatness thus tending directly to develop superiority in our own minds. This is the path to mental greatness, but it is so simple that few have found it.

When we think about life we should always view the sunny side of personal existence and the real life of interior existence. Instead of viewing life as a burden or as a misery to be endured now, that glory may come in the future, we should think of the unbounded possibilities that real life has in store here and now. Our mind should be concerned with the real life itself and should seek to form the very highest conceptions possible of such a life. There is no greater subject for thought than life when we look at life as an eternity of rich and marvelous possibilities. And to view life in this way will not only elevate and enlarge the mind, but will also give us the conscious realization of a continuous increase in life. And as life increases everything in mind and personality will increase to correspond. A great life produces a great mind and a high soul, but to attain the greater life we must enlarge our view of life. And this we do by turning all attention upon real life itself, and the marvelous possibilities of real life. Realizing these facts we should never think of that which is small when we have the capacity to think of that which is great. And we all can think of the great. There is a beautiful and a wonderful side to all life, and the possibilities of all life are unbounded. We therefore understand the value of training ourselves to take the correct view of life, for to think of the larger and the more beautiful side of all life is to enlarge and beautify the life that is in us.

The same principle should be observed in all our thought about nature, and to learn how to enter into that perfect communion with nature where we can see her real beauty and her wonderful power, is to apply a faculty that deserves the highest state of cultivation in every mind. Those mental conceptions that are formed while we are in perfect touch with the true in nature are of exceptional worth and will add largely to the power and superiority of mind. Therefore when we think of nature all attention should be concentrated upon the ideal, the beautiful and true side. When we see what may seem to be flaws it is wisdom to pass them by and never permit them to impress our minds. Even a weed should be thought of with respect because it is also a product of natural law, and it is our privilege to transform the weed into something that has real beauty and worth. But here it is highly important to remember that our power to perfect anything in nature can only increase as we think less of its flaws and more of its hidden splendors.

When we come to the subject of our own personal life and experiences we cannot apply too well the principle of scientific thinking, because what we think of the experiences of to-day will largely determine what experiences we are to have to-morrow. What we receive from life passes through the channel of experience and every channel tends to modify that which passes through. The subject therefore is vitally important. As frequently stated before, scientific thinking is thinking that produces the larger, the better, the greater and the superior; thinking that promotes progress; thinking that produces results. And such thinking is scientific because it is in harmony with the purpose of life which is to advance constantly in the producing of greater and greater results; consequently to think scientifically about experience every mental conception formed by experience should be formed in the likeness of those facts that will be found back of the experience. Every experience can teach us something we do not know; therefore instead of deploring the experience we should receive it with joy and proceed at once to look for the truth it has come to convey. No experience will be unpleasant if we meet it with the one desire to know what it has to teach; and what is better still when we think of experience as a messenger of truth we will form only lofty mental conceptions of all experience. We will thus not only gain much new truth, but we will enrich the mind with these many superior conceptions. In the usual way we meet unpleasant experiences with a heavy heart, and we meet the pleasant ones with the thought of personal gratification. Those mental conceptions that we form while thinking of our experiences in the usual way will therefore be ordinary and frequently detrimental. In the meantime, the new truth that those experiences could have conveyed will remain unlearned and undiscovered.

The reverses and misfortunes of life are usually looked upon with regret, and are deplored as so many obstacles in our way, but such thought is not conducive to good results. Reverses come because we have failed to comply with the laws of life, therefore instead of regretting

it has come to ...
will be unpleasant if ...
one desire to know w...
and what is better w...
experience as a mea...
will form only lofty ...
of all experience. W...
gain much new truth ...
the mind with these ...
ceptions. In the usu...
pleasant experiences ...
and we meet the plea...
thought of personal g...
mental conceptions t...
thinking of our exper...
way will therefore be ...
quently detrimental. ...
the new truth that ...
could have conveyed ...
learned and undiscov...

The reverses and ...
are usually looked upo...
are deplored as so m...
way, but such thought ...
to good results. Rev...
we have failed to ...
of life, therefore ...

the experience we should use it as a means of finding wherein we have failed. And having done this we may proceed once more with the positive assurance of gaining increased success. Misfortunes may also be employed as builders of character because there is nothing that strengthens the mind and the soul so much as to pass through reverses without being mentally or morally disturbed. The spiritual giant can pass through anything and gain good from anything. To him misfortunes are not disagreeable; they are simply opportunities to bring out greater life and power, to learn more laws, to gain a better understanding of things, and thus achieve still greater things when the next attempt is made. But though we may not have attained such a lofty state we can at least pass through reverses with our minds fixed constantly upon the high goal in view. The result will be greater moral stability, greater mental power and the turning of fate in the direction we ourselves desire to move.

That knowledge and power is gained through pain is a well known belief and it is one of those beliefs that contains much truth; and it is also true that when we have learned the lesson the pain came to teach the pain disappears. When the pain is felt attention should at once be directed upon that finer and larger life that lies back of the personal man. We feel pain because the outer forces are not in harmony with the more perfect life within; therefore to remove the pain this harmony must be restored. To restore this harmony we should proceed to gain consciousness of the finer forces of the inner life because when we become conscious of the inner life, which is always in harmony, the disorder of the outer life will disappear. The more we think of the pain the more conscious we become of the discord in the outer life and the more difficult it becomes to gain consciousness of the harmony of the inner life. Therefore to think scientifically about pain is to take the mind beyond pain into the inner realms of life where perfect harmony reigns. The result will be freedom from pain and the discovery of a new interior world. When we take this higher view of pain, reverses, misfortune, troubles and the like we gradually work ourselves out of the lower and the confused, and will ere long get out of them entirely. It is therefore evident that when we think scientifically about the ills of life we proceed directly to rise above them and will therefore meet them no more This is perfectly natural because when your thoughts are high you will rise in the scale; you will leave behind the inferior and the wrong and you will enter into the possession of the superior and the right.

When we think about ourselves we should always think about the unlimited possibilities of the within. Attention should be directed upon the larger self, and every thought should be formed in the likeness of the highest mental conceptions that we can form of the superior. We may, however, recognize the existence of flaws in our nature; in fact, it is necessary to know where the weak places are in order to remove them; but the mind should never hold its attention upon those weak places. The mental eye should never look upon the imperfect, but should look through it and direct its vision towards the ideal. And here we find the reason why the average person does not improve as he should. The fact is he thinks of himself as he appears to be in the limited personal self. He patterns his thought after the small life that he can see in the outer self. And as man is as he thinks he will therefore not rise above the quality or the nature of his own thought. No one can rise any higher than his thoughts. Therefore, so long as your thoughts are like your present limited personal life you will never become any more than you are now. The mind, however, that transcends its present states, talents and qualities and tries to gain mental conceptions of the larger and the superior will steadily rise and become as large as those new conceptions that have been formed, and may later rise still higher thus reaching greater heights of consciousness, ability, and power than was dreamed of before.

In the world of feeling the thorough application of the law of scientific thought is extremely important, the reason being that we generally live upon those planes where our feelings are the strongest. All our feelings therefore should be transformed to the highest planes of thought and living that we can possibly think of. But since feelings deal principally with forces, whether in mind or personality, it is in the world of force that we shall have to direct our attention if a change of feeling is to be made. And this is done very simply by training the mind to always try to feel the finer and the more powerful forces that are back of every state, condition or action. Whenever anything takes place in your system try to feel the finer forces in that part of the system where the action is taking place. This experience may not give you any new sensation at first, but you will gradually become conscious of a whole universe of finer life and action within yourself. Then your mind will be living in a much larger world and in a much richer world. These finer life forces that you feel within yourself are the powerful creative energies of the subconscious, and it is these energies that are so valuable in the development of the mind and the reconstruction of the body. Therefore, whenever you exercise the sense of feeling try to feel the higher and the finer that is in you. You will soon succeed and the results will not only add enjoyments, both to mind and personality, but will also give you the mastery of new and powerful forces.

An expanding and ascending desire should be back of every action of the mind, and all efforts to gain the conscious realization of the new should aim at the very largest mental scope and realization possible. Every desire should desire the largest, the purest, the most refined and the most perfect expression that present mental capacity can be conscious of. This will add remarkably to the joy of living and will have a refining effect upon the entire system. The most refined expressions of desire give the greatest pleasure, whether the channel of expression be physical, mental or spiritual. But no desire should be destroyed. The proper course is to refine it and turn it into channels through which the forces back of that desire can be wisely employed now. When we refine our desires those desires will never lead us into wrongs or temptations because the fact is that a refined desire never desires to do wrong. On the contrary, every desire that desires higher and higher expressions will, through such a desire, tend to enter into the right, the more perfect and the superior. In this connection, we should remember that all ascending actions are right actions, that all descending actions are wrong actions, and that this is the only difference between right and wrong.

Every mental aim should have the greater in view, and every plan that is formed should embody the largest possibilities conceivable. Too many minds fail because their plans are so small and their aims too low; but the larger and the higher is invariably the purpose of scientific thought—thought that thinks for results. Every mental force, therefore, should be an aspiring force and should have the power to spur us on to greater efforts and higher goals. This is extremely important as we shall know when we learn that all forces are creative. When all the forces of your system are trained to aspire, everything that is being created in your system will be created more perfectly and you will steadily advance. In like manner, when every mental action is constructive, everything that may be placed in action in your mind will tend to build you up and will tend to work for the purpose you have in view. Mental actions that have no particular aim are usually destructive, but every action of the mind can be made constructive if we make it a point to always think for results. The first step in this connection, and the only really important step, is to have a strong desire for mental construction constantly held in mind, and to give this desire increased attention when our mental actions are especially strong. In all our efforts our object should be greater things, and to realize this object no building power in mind or personality must be idle or misdirected. On the contrary, everything within us should be trained to work for all those definite results that we have in view, and all actions of mind and body should be so perfectly directed upon the production of those results that everything we do under any

circumstance will tend to work con-
stantly and directly for those results. It
is when we proceed in this manner that
our thinking is right, designed and scien-
tific, and it is such thinking alone that
we can employ when we aim to think for
results.

O make the right use of thought we must make it a practice to think that which is inherently true. Therefore whatever we think about we must formulate our thoughts according to the truth which we know to exist within that of which we think. When we think about life we must think of life as it is in itself and not as it appears to be in the personal existence of some one who does not know how to use life. There are people who make life a burden, but life in itself is anything but a burden. On the contrary it is a rare privilege. Therefore, to think of life as a burden is to take the wrong view of life. It is to think the untruth about life. It is to view life from the standpoint of one who has misapplied life. Accordingly what we judge is not life, but a mistaken opinion about life. Our thought in the matter will thus be foreign to life and will naturally mislead us when we try to

apply it in connection with real living.

When we think about life we must think about real life and not about some illusion that we might have of life. The average person's thought about life, however, is simply an opinion about his misunderstanding about life and therefore his thinking is never designed, constructive nor scientific Life itself is a joy, a rich blessing and it means so much that an eternity of mental growth will be required to comprehend its entire meaning. Life is not something that comes and goes; it is something that always is. Neither is life something that can be produced or destroyed. Life is inexhaustible and indestructible and contains within itself a definite and eternal purpose. We should therefore view life according to this idea. And when we gain this right idea of life we can become more deeply conscious of real life and thus gain possession of more life. This is extremely important because it is only as we gain added life that we can gain added ability and power. When we gain a correct conception of life we also enter into harmony with the purpose of life which means to enter the path of continuous advancement along all lines, the result of which will be perpetually increased in all things.

When you think about yourself view yourself as you are at your best and not as you appear when in the midst of failure. You never fail when you are at your best and you are true to yourself only when you are at your best. Therefore if you wish to think the truth about yourself think about yourself as you are when you are true to yourself and not as you appear to be when you are false to yourself. Scientific thinking does not recognize weakness of mind or body because you yourself are not weak, and you would never feel weak if you were always true to yourself. Thoughts should never be formed in the likeness of a weak condition because such thinkmg will perpetuate the condition of weakness. When weakness is felt think the truth about yourself; that is, that you are inherently strong and the weakness will disappear. Form your thought in the likeness of yourself as you are in your real and larger self; that is, as you are when you are true to your whole self—full of life, strength and vigor. And your thought will become the thought of strength conveying strength to every part of your system.

In the right use of thought we never permit ourselves to say that we cannot. On the contrary we continue to believe and say, "I can do whatever I undertake to do and I am equal to every occasion." This is our firm conviction when we have come to that place where we really know what is in us, and it is a conviction that is based upon actual scientific fact. Unlimited possibilities are latent in every mind; therefore man is inherently equal to every occasion and he should claim his whole power at all times. If he does not make himself equal to every occasion the cause is that he fails to express all that is in him. But the greater capacity that is within anyone cannot fully express itself so long as thought is created in the likeness of weakness, doubt and limitations. Therefore the right and scientific use of thought becomes the direct channel through which the greatness that is within man may come forth and. act in real life.

Man is not naturally in the hands of fate for the truth is that fate is in the hands of man. Man may appear to be controlled by a destiny that seems distinct from himself, but the real truth is that he himself has created the very life and the very tendency of that destiny. The destiny of every man in his own creation, be it good or otherwise, but so long as he thinks he is in the hands of this destiny he will fail to intelligently employ his own creations, and will accordingly originate adverse circumstances. Many have speculated as to the real cause of adverse circumstances, bad luck and the like, but the cause is simply this, that when man finds himself in adversity he has neglected to direct, consciously and intelligently, the forces which he himself has placed in action; and this neglect can invariably be traced to the belief that we are all controlled more or less by what we call fate. For this reason the sooner we eliminate that belief absolutely the better.

No man will attempt to control the

forces of life so long as he thinks he is unavoidably controlled by those forces; but if those forces are not intelligently controlled, their action will be aimless and we shall have that confusion which is otherwise termed adversity. Every word, every thought and every action gives expression to certain life forces, and what those forces will do depends first upon their original nature and second upon how they are directed in their courses. The sum total of all the words, thoughts and actions expressed by man will constitute the forces of his destiny, and the result of those forces will constitute his fate. What those forces are in the beginning depends upon what man created them to be, and what those forces will unitedly produce will depend upon whether they are directed by man himself or left to act aimlessly. But man can make his words, thoughts and actions what he wishes them to be. He can direct them intelligently into channels of constructive and perpetual growth. It is therefore simply understood how man is unconsciously the cause of his fate, and how he can consciously and intelligently create his own fate. To create his own fate, however, he must make the right use of thought; that is, he must think for results.

To think scientifically about the people we meet it is necessary to apply the same principle which we apply to our true thought about life. We must think of people as they are in themselves and not as they appear to be while out of harmony with existence. When we are judging man we should judge the real man and not his mistakes. The mistakes of the man do not constitute the man any more than the absence of light constitutes light. The usual way, however, of judging man is to look at his weak points and then after comparing these with his strong points call the result the man himself. But this is as unscientific as to combine black with white and speak of the result as pure white. The weaknesses that we find in man may disappear in a day. They frequently do, while his virtues and superior qualities may double in power at any time. Then we have another man, and we say he has changed, which is not strictly true. The real man has not changed. The real man is already unbounded in life and power and does not have to change. The change that we see is simply this, that more of the true worth of his real being has been expressed.

Our thoughts about other people are more or less deeply impressed upon our own minds; therefore we cannot afford to think anything wrong about anybody. The better we understand life the more convinced we become that the average person is doing the best he knows how. For this reason we shall be training our minds to think the whole truth about the human race when we take this view, and what is highly important, such a view will tend to keep our own minds wholesome and clean. Then when we add to this the larger view of man himself, in his true glory and power, our thought about man will become as we wish it to be, strictly scientific.

In thinking for results all circumstances should be viewed as opportunities because that is what they are in reality. And to think correctly we must think of things according to what there really is in them. No circumstance is actually against us though we may go against a circumstance and thus produce a clash. A circumstance is usually similar to an electrical force. It may destroy or it may serve depending upon how it is approached. The power, however, is there and we are the ones to determine what that power is to do. Our relation to anything in the external depends upon how we view the circumstances involved. When we think of circumstances as adverse we become antagonistic to those circumstances and in consequence produce discord, trouble and misfortune. But when we think of circumstances as opportunities to take advantage of and control, we relate ourselves harmoniously to the power that is contained in those circumstances. Thus by entering into harmony with that power we will perpetuate more and more of it until we have made it our own altogether.

When disappointments appear it is not scientific to feel depressed nor to view the experience as a misfortune. To the advancing mind a disappointment is always an open door to something better. When you fail to get what you want there is something better at hand for you; that is, if you are moving forward. Therefore to every advancing mind so called disappointments may be viewed as prophecies of better things. If you are not moving forward a disappointment indicates that you have not made yourself equal to your ideal. But the fact that you have felt disappointment proves that you have seen the ideal, and to see an ideal indicates that that ideal is within your reach ready for you to possess if you will press forward steadily and surely until the goal is reached. Therefore no matter what your condition may be in life a disappointment indicates that there is something better at hand for you if you will go and work for it. For this reason, instead of feeling depressed you should rejoice, and then press on with more faith and enthusiasm than ever that you may meet your own at the earliest possible moment

These thoughts are not presented simply to give encouragement or cheer. The fact is they are thoroughly scientific and based upon two well established laws in metaphysics. The first law is that no person can feel disappointed unless he has had a perception of something better. And the second law is that whoever is far enough advanced to perceive the better has the capacity to acquire that something better, though he must make full use of the power at hand. Too many minds that see the ideal simply dream about it and feel depressed because the ideal has not been reached, while in the meantime they do nothing to work themselves up to that ideal. Instead such minds should take a scientific view of the entire subject and then press on towards the goal before them. They positively will succeed.

When we look upon a disappointment as a misfortune the depressed thought that follows will take us down and away from the open door of the better things, and will in consequence prevent us from realizing the greater good which was in store. We shall then have to give much time and effort to the bringing of ourselves back again to the gates of the ideal we had in view. But such tactics we cannot afford to employ if our object is to work and think for results. We conclude therefore that whatever comes or does not come the best way is always to smile and press on.

It is scientific to recognize only the sunny side of everything and to expect only the best results from every effort, because the sunny side is the real side and the substantial side, and our thinking should be concerned only with the substantial, or with that which has real or possible worth. Failure is an empty place, so to speak, or a condition involving a group of misdirected actions. To think of failure therefore is to produce a mental tendency towards misdirected or abortive actions, and at the same time create thoughts that waste energy. To dwell mentally on the sunny side, however, is to turn all the actions of the mind towards the construction of greater worth in the mind; and accordingly the habit of dwelling upon the sunny side will invariably tend to develop brilliancy of mind, clearness of thought and greater intellectual capacity. The principal reason for this is found in the fact that such a mind deals almost entirely with the larger, the greater and the limitless of the potential. Mind therefore naturally expands and develops and steadily gains in power, comprehension and lucidity along all lines. To act in harmony with this principle we should expect the best results from every effort because the best results do exist potentially in every effort; and to be scientific we must think of things as they really are in themselves and not as they appear while in the hands of the incompetent. It is not our purpose to dwell mentally upon the absence of results, but to give all our thought and attention to the right use of those powers within us that actually can produce results.

To think scientifically about the health and the wholeness of mind and body is one of the most important essentials of all because health is indispensable to the highest attainments and the greatest achievements. The principle, however, is that the real man is well, and that you yourself are the real man. When you are thinking about yourself as you really are and since you, the real YOU, the individuality, are always well, your thought of yourself is not right and constructive unless you think of yourself as absolutely and permanently well. Every condition in the personal man is the result of habits of thought. Therefore when you think of yourself as being absolutely and permanently well you will through that mode of thinking give absolute and permanent health to the entire system. This is a law that is as strong as life itself. And we are not making extravagant statements when we declare that if this law were universally employed disease would be practically banished from off the face of the earth. This law is the absolute truth and every student of modern metaphysics knows that it is the truth. That its power is invincible no one can deny. Therefore the wise course to pursue is to apply this law thoroughly under all sorts of circumstances and never lose faith in its effectiveness for a moment.

In training ourselves to think for results we must constantly bear in mind the great fact that man invariably grows into the likeness of that which he thinks of the most. Therefore, think constantly of what you want to become and your life will daily grow in that direction. Think constantly of health, power, ability, capacity, worth and superiority and the powers of your being will gradually and steadily produce all those qualities in your own system. But all such thinking must be deep, persistent and of the heart. It is that thinking which is in touch with the under currents of life that shapes human destiny; therefore all such thinking should always be as we wish to become. No thoughts should ever enter the mind that do not contain in the ideal the very things that we wish to attain or accomplish in the real. But to train ourselves in this mode of thinking is not difficult. It is only a matter of deciding what we want in life; then to think the most of those things and make such thinking deep, persistent, positive and strong.

O train the mind to think for results there are four essentials that must be provided. The first is to carry on all thinking in the attitude of right mental states. The second is to think only such thoughts as will push your work and that will constantly promote your present purpose in life. The third is to employ only such creative processes in the mind as will tend directly to produce the larger, the better and the superior. And the fourth is to think only the real truth about all things; that is, to fashion all thought according to the most perfect mental conception that can be formed of the real in everything of which we may think. The first three essentials have been fully considered in the preceding pages. We shall therefore conclude by giving our attention to the fourth. And in doing so we must prepare ourselves for thought that is somewhat deeper than the usual.

To begin we must realize that there is a vast difference between what seems to be true and what really is true, and that all thinking to be right, wholesome, constructive and scientific must deal directly with that which really is true. To illustrate we will consider the being of man. Viewed externally man seems to have many imperfections, to be limited in all things and to be more or less in the hands of fate. But when we consider, not the present conditions of the personal man, but the possibilities of his marvelous interior nature, we find that imperfections are simply greater things in the process of development. We find that there is no limit to his power and inherent capacity, and we find that he is strong enough, if he applies all his strength, to overcome any fate, to change any circumstance and to positively determine his own destiny.

When we examine other things we find the same to be true; that is, that there is more in everything than what appears on the surface. And therefore what appears to be true of things when viewed externally is not the whole truth; in fact, it may frequently be the very opposite of the real truth. The right use of thought, however, must concern itself with the real truth, or the inside facts in the case; therefore, in thinking for results we must — fashion our thoughts according to what really is in those thoughts of which we may be thinking.

In dealing with the inside facts of any case, condition or object the question always is: "What are the possibilities; what can be done with what is in the thing; and what results can be gained from the full use of everything that this circumstance or that object may contain?" And it is highly important to answer this question as fully and as correctly as possible because we are as we think and our thoughts are always like the things we think about. Besides we must be conscious of the real interior possibility of those things with which we deal in order to secure the greatest results. If we think only of the imperfections and the limitations that appear on the surface our thinking will be inferior, and we will become ordinary both in mind and personality. But if we think of what is really true of the greater possibilities of all things we will think far greater thoughts, and we will think inspiring thoughts—thoughts that will stir the mind to greater ambition and greater achievement, and the mind will accordingly enter more and more into a larger, greater and richer world. In consequence our mental powers along all lines will steadily increase.

To think what is really true about all things is therefore to think of the greater powers and possibilities that are in all things; and to think the truth in the broadest sense is to direct the mind upon the whole of life, with all its possibilities, and to deal mentally with all the richness, all the power and all the marvelousness that can be discerned in everything pertaining to life. Or to state it briefly, you have begun to think what is really true when your mind has begun to move constantly towards the vastness of the greater things that lie before us. And here we must remember that there is no end to that vastness; no limit to the greatness that is inherent in life. Therefore, we may go on and on indefinitely thinking more and more truth about everything; and as we do we shall continue to enrich and enlarge both the talents and the powers of the mind.

It is therefore evident that when we think the truth about all things, that is, think of what is really possible in all things, we will cause the mind to enlarge and expand constantly, because as we think of the larger we invariably enlarge the mind. And the real truth about all things grows larger and larger the further we advance in the pursuit of truth. And the importance of such a mode of thinking becomes more and more evident as we realize that an ever enlarging mind is an absolute necessity if our aim is to think for results.

When we proceed to think the truth about things we naturally think of the true state of affairs within those things. We think of the power itself and not of its past use. Therefore, such thinking will invariably keep the mind in a wholesome and harmonious condition. That which is true of the real nature of things must be good and wholesome, and therefore to think of that which is true must necessarily produce wholesome conditions in the mind. And here it is well to emphasize the fact that the mind that is wholesome and harmonious is far more powerful than the mind that is not. Such a mind therefore may secure far greater results, no matter what its work or purpose may be.

To think what is really true about everything will for the same reason prevent the formation of detrimental and perverted states of mind, and will also prevent the misdirection of mental energy. This is a fact of great importance to those who aim for results, because in the average mind the majority of the energies placed in action are either misdirected or applied in such a way as to be of no permanent value. Another fact that needs emphasis in this connection is that the thinking of truth will tend to bring out all that is in us. And the reason is that when we think of what there really is in everything the mind becomes more penetrating as well as more comprehensive in its scope of action. The result therefore will naturally be that our own mental actions will penetrate more and more every element and power that is in us, and thus arouse more and more of everything that is in us. In other words, the mind will proceed to act positively upon everything that exists in the vast domain of our own mental world, conscious and subconscious, and will actually think into activity every power and faculty we possess.

When we think the real truth about everything in life, including our own self, we invariably focus attention upon the best, the largest and the richest that exists in everything. And this we must do if our purpose is to secure greater and better results the further we go in our progress toward attainment and achievement. Your mind, your thought, your ability, your power, in brief, everything of worth in your system, cannot be fully and effectively applied unless your attention is constantly concentrated upon the greater; unless you are mentally moving towards the greater; unless you are giving your whole life and power to the greater; and to this end your attention must constantly be focused upon the best and the greatest that you can possibly picture in your mind.

When you think the truth you think of what can be done. You do not think of weakness, obstacles or possible failure; nor do you consider what may be dark, adverse or detrimental in your present circumstances. Instead you think of the tremendous power that is within you, and you try to turn on the full current of that power so that what you want to accomplish positively will be accomplished. But in turning on that full current you make a special effort to make every action in your system constructive, whether it be physical or mental, because in working for results you want all that is in you to work thoroughly, continuously and directly for those self same results. We realize therefore the importance of training the mind to think the truth according to this larger view of the truth in order that the best use, the fullest use and the most effective use of every power of mind and thought may be applied; and we shall find as we proceed that the art of thinking the truth in this manner can be readily mastered by anyone whose desire is to make his life as large, as rich and as perfect as life can be made.

To restate the principles and ideas upon which the right use of the mind is based.we need simply return to the four essentials mentioned in the beginning of this chapter. We proceed by placing the mind in certain mental states called right mental states because the mind has more power while acting in such states, and can act more effectively while acting through the wholesome constructive attitudes of those states. We continue by thinking only such thoughts as will tend to work with us, and give their full force to the promotion of our purpose. We avoid thoughts and mental states that are against us and permit only those that are positively and absolutely for us. We place in action only such mental processes as tend to create the larger, the better and the superior in ourselves because our object is not simply to secure results now, but to secure greater and greater results; and to promote this object we must constantly develop the larger, the better and the superior in ourselves. Lastly we make it a special point to think the real truth about all things; that is, we form our mental conceptions, our ideas and our thoughts in the exact likeness of the great, the marvelous and the limitless that is inherent in all life.

We aim to fashion our thoughts according to everything that is great, lofty and of superior worth so that we may think great thoughts because we are as we think. When our thoughts are small we will become small, weak and inefficient; but when our thoughts are great we will become great, powerful and efficient. This is the law, and as we apply this law as fully and as effectively as we possibly can, we shall positively become much and achieve much, and the object we have in view—the securing of greater and greater results—will be realized. Therefore in all our thinking we focus all the actions of mind upon the unbounded possibilities that are inherent in ourselves, that are inherent in all things, that are inherent in the vastness of the cosmos. We turn all our thoughts upon the rich, the limitless and the sublime so that we may live constantly in a larger and superior mental world—a world that we are determined to make larger and larger every day. And as we live, think and work in that ever-growing mental world we insist that everything we do shall, with a certainty, build for that greater future we now have in view; and that every action of mind and body shall be a positive force moving steadily, surely and perpetually towards those sublime heights of attainment and achievement that we have longed for so much while inspired by the spirit of ambition's lofty dream.

Made in the USA
Middletown, DE
25 September 2021